# MY BOOK OF LIFE

COMPANION BOOK FOR

THE GUARDIAN CODE:

*It's Not Your Fault [And I Can Prove It!]*


STEVE SHENK

PUBLISHED BY FIDELI PUBLISHING INC.

ISBN: 978-1-60414-729-2

COMPANION BOOKS:

*THE GUARDIAN CODE:*
*It's Not Your Fault [And I Can Prove It!]*

*THE BEST OF*
*THE GUARDIAN CODE*

# Introduction

My Book of Life is a small, pocket-sized, daily-use companion journal to the *THE GUARDIAN CODE* magic gift textbook. My assignment, which I have chosen to accept, is to perform the daily exercises in this little journal for a period of six months.

When the first six-month journal is completed I will then refresh and renew my commitments, objectives, and targeted accomplishments for the next six months. I will continue filling six-month journal after journal, creating my future and documenting the path of my exciting life until creation is no longer desired.

I know that if I take a little time each day to create my future, documenting what I have experienced and learned, I will fill my life with happiness, joy, and unimagined abundance and prosperity. My Book of Life will ultimately read as a great adventure to both myself and those who follow me as the students of the teacher they are ready to have appear.

*My Book of Life* is made up of three sections or "tools" of creation:

1. **My Gratitude Journal** is the tool by which all negative thoughts, doubt, fear, and 'un-creation' can be controlled and eliminated. Virtually all of the true principles taught in *THE GUARDIAN CODE* textbook are implemented through this magnificent, all-encompassing principle.

2. **The My Creation Journal** is the creative tool by which I turn "thoughts into things." After I have listed all of the objectives or targets I wish to obtain and achieve, I will follow this simple system of affirming visualizations for each desired item "as if" it has already been achieved or is in my possession. I have learned that every thought creates its physical form when I put out a clear statement and mental (creative) picture of it already being in existence. I am following the instructions in this journal to create my future "as if" it already exists.

3. **My Journal of Knowledge and Reports** is documentation, essentially a diary, of the knowledge and understanding I have obtained along with my targets achieved. This is a chronicle of the rewards I have received by

practicing the creative principles that I have learned. As I read and remind myself of what I have accomplished, I build an even more powerful belief in who I am and my power to be master of my destiny. The reports in this journal tell me how well I'm doing at consistently performing my daily creative exercises. By recording my actions each day I am accountable to myself for the results I achieve.

# GRATITUDE

## My Gratitude Journal

My Gratitude Journal is the key by which I create my life of greatness, peace and happiness.

As I have studied and learned the lessons taught by the Guardian in the book, *THE GUARDIAN CODE: It's Not Your Fault [And I Can Prove It!]* I have learned that I can take back my power over how all of the uncontrollable circumstances in life affect me by applying the principles (natural universal laws) of absolute truth. I have learned I am a very powerful creator, and that every thought creates. With this creative power, the only reason that everything in my life is not what I want it to be is that I, along with virtually everyone else, "un-create" with thoughts of doubt, fear, guilt, jealousy, and denial of the power and greatness within.

When I choose to use my creative power to think of (create) and visualize my desired objectives **without "un-creating,"** that which I focus my thoughts on is created. I then draw unlimited supply from the endless universe.

---

*If every thought creates, whether positive or negative, then "successful people" simply create with positive thoughts a bit more than they " un-create" with negative thoughts. Think about it.*

— The Guardian

---

The Guardian has stated that gratitude is the tool that will enable me to apply every law that " just is." I know that it is impossible to think of lack (not having enough) and gratitude at the same time. I can't think discouragement and gratitude at the same time. Jealousy and gratitude don't go together. Greed and gratitude are opposites. So here is my conclusion. Every single negative, doubtful, un-creating thought can be offset and neutralized with gratitude. Very simply, as I create and eliminate "un-creating" by applying gratitude, my life is full of joy, abundance, and peace of mind.

## My Gratitude Journal

This Journal is my summary of that for which I am grateful.

I have listed several categories of Gratitudes. I have left some pages for additional categories that will come to mind later. I have handwritten five items in each category. As I think of more items I can overflow to the back of the page on which that category is listed.

As I rewrite my gratitude list at the beginning of each six-month *My Book of Life* journal, I adjust the items to reflect my present life conditions.

I have underlined the 10 items on my gratitude list that I choose to read every morning before I start my day and before I begin stating and visualizing the objectives I create in my life.

I use my gratitude journal portion of my book of life to eliminate fear, doubt, discouragement, anger, jealousy, envy, arrogance, and judgmentalism, and, in fact, to purge all "un-creation" from my life.

# My Plan

1. I read all my gratitudes (out loud if possible) with strong thought and feeling at the beginning of each week.

2. Each morning I read, out loud, my 10 favorite, underlined gratitudes. I also add to this list any other gratitudes needed for that day.

3. When I read out loud and visualize each objective in the creation portion of this book of life I express gratitude for already possessing it.

4. When I experience any negative, doubtful, or discouraging thought or emotion (un-creation) I immediately read every gratitude that refutes or neutralizes it. I always remember that it is impossible to stay negative (un-creation) and express gratitude (creation) at the same time.

---

*When you experience discouragement, anger, worry, or unhappiness, please accept the challenge to list five gratitudes that are associated with the subject of concern. I guarantee that you will be unable to stay negative. Think about it.*

— The Guardian

# GRATITUDES LIST

Below I have listed at least five of my gratitudes for each category.

I am grateful for living people:

I am grateful for people no longer living:

Gratitudes for my physical strengths:

Gratitudes for my mental and emotional strengths:

Gratitudes regarding my work:

Gratitudes regarding my possessions:

Gratitudes for the things of Nature:

Gratitudes for places on earth:

Gratitudes for modern inventions:

Gratitudes for foods I enjoy:

My Own Special Gratitudes:

Gratitudes for my spiritual progress:

Gratitudes—to be completed upon finishing this six-month **My Book of Life Journal**—for my accomplishments for this six-month period in *My Book of Life:*

# My Creation Journal

Instructions for my creation of the qualities, objectives, possessions, and relationships that I choose to have complete the makeup of my whole physical, mental, emotional, and spiritual self, along with the environment and possessions of my joyful and exciting life.

---

*Normally this would be referred to as the "goal setting" section. Unfortunately, goal lists as they are presently taught, do not work for most people since they usually involve planning HOW to reach the "goals" which unfortunately establishes doubt, "un-creating" the objective immediately. Think about it.*

— The Guardian

If instead of the terms OBJECTIVE or GOAL, I also use the term **TARGET** for that which I choose to achieve or obtain, my creative power can be more perfectly engaged.

- Here is my list of objectives (TARGETS).
- All entries are written in my own handwriting and stated as being already achieved.
- My list includes everything I choose to be, have, and accomplish, with no limits on the possibility or the number of TARGETS.
- I know that it's impossible to think lack and gratitude at the same time. Therefore, I focus only on **gratitude** for each of these, which eliminates the "un-creation" of doubt, disbelief, and discouragement.

---

*The most powerful prayer is one of gratitude for the possession of that which is needed or desired. Think about it.*

— The Guardian

## The application of my ultimate creative power.

Below is my list of qualities, objectives, possessions and relationships, which I draw from the unlimited supply of the universe.

I have listed every desire and need, placing no limits on possibility of achievement or number of objectives.

I never plan HOW to achieve my objectives, only focusing on the WHY. I never ask the following three questions:

"Can I see myself accomplishing this?"
"What do I have to give up for this?"
"What are the chances of my success?"

These objectives and achievements ***are already mine.*** I simply release them into my presence and possession by reading them out loud twice daily, morning and evening. Using as many of the five senses as possible (sight, hearing, smell, touch, and taste) I visualize how it *feels* to gratefully have them.

**Example:** "All of my financial obligations are paid. I am completely debt-free with a savings account of $5,000."

**Example:** "I am in a fun, exciting, loving, committed relationship with my companion who is..."

My two per day repetition of objectives will be very effective. However, if I take the time to write them down and repeat them to myself often in front of the mirror, I will ehnhance my creative power in ways I've never known.

After I complete my visualizations I turn to my Journal of Knowledge and Reports section.

1.

2.

3.

4.

5.

6.

7. ______________________________

8. ______________________________

9. ______________________________

10. ______________________________

11. ______________________________

12. ______________________________

13.

14.

15.

16.

17.

18.

19. ______________________________

______________________________

______________________________

______________________________

20. ______________________________

______________________________

______________________________

______________________________

21. ______________________________

______________________________

______________________________

______________________________

22. ______________________________

______________________________

______________________________

______________________________

23. ______________________________

______________________________

______________________________

______________________________

24. ______________________________

______________________________

______________________________

______________________________

25.

26.

27.

28.

29.

30.

31. _____

32. _____

33. _____

34. _____

35. _____

36. _____

# My Journal of Knowledge and Reports

I am a student, ready for my teacher to appear, and that which I learn I gladly teach to the next student from this, my Journal of Knowledge and Reports.

I have reported, here, each date on which I have completed reading and visualizing (in gratitude) my TARGETS—both morning and evening.

I have written a "new" thought each day. Some days there are small changes in attitude. Some days there is just a happy "positive" observation like, "the sunrise was beautiful" or "I got a hug today." Other days I record great new understandings. There are other exciting accounts of my receiving inspiration or when a path toward one of my Targets has been opened for me, I am grateful for and reread (re-experience) all of this wisdom and goodness at least once each month for the six-month duration of this Journal.

*Folks typically forget 80% of what they learn each day. 'Relearning' will help you retain what has been learned more permanently. Think about it.*

— The Guardian

Date: ________________ Completed 1 ( ) 2 ( )

Visualizations: ________________________________

Today's thought: ________________________________

________________________________________________

________________________________________________

Date: ________________ Completed 1 ( ) 2 ( )

Visualizations: ________________________________

Today's thought: ________________________________

________________________________________________

________________________________________________

Date: ________________ Completed 1 ( ) 2 ( )

Visualizations: ________________________________

Today's thought: ________________________________

________________________________________________

________________________________________________

Date: ________________ Completed 1 ( ) 2 ( )

Visualizations: ________________________________

Today's thought: ________________________________

________________________________________________

________________________________________________

Date: ________________ Completed 1 ( ) 2 ( )

Visualizations: ________________

Today's thought: ________________

________________

________________

Date: ________________ Completed 1 ( ) 2 ( )

Visualizations: ________________

Today's thought: ________________

________________

________________

Date: ________________ Completed 1 ( ) 2 ( )

Visualizations: ________________

Today's thought: ________________

________________

________________

Date: ________________ Completed 1 ( ) 2 ( )

Visualizations: ________________

Today's thought: ________________

________________

________________

Date: ____________ Completed 1 ( ) 2 ( )

Visualizations: ____________

Today's thought: ____________

____________

____________

Date: ____________ Completed 1 ( ) 2 ( )

Visualizations: ____________

Today's thought: ____________

____________

____________

Date: ____________ Completed 1 ( ) 2 ( )

Visualizations: ____________

Today's thought: ____________

____________

____________

Date: ____________ Completed 1 ( ) 2 ( )

Visualizations: ____________

Today's thought: ____________

____________

____________

Date: ________________ Completed 1 ( ) 2 ( )

Visualizations: ____________________________

Today's thought: ____________________________

____________________________________________

____________________________________________

Date: ________________ Completed 1 ( ) 2 ( )

Visualizations: ____________________________

Today's thought: ____________________________

____________________________________________

____________________________________________

Date: ________________ Completed 1 ( ) 2 ( )

Visualizations: ____________________________

Today's thought: ____________________________

____________________________________________

____________________________________________

Date: ________________ Completed 1 ( ) 2 ( )

Visualizations: ____________________________

Today's thought: ____________________________

____________________________________________

____________________________________________

Date: ______________ Completed 1 ( ) 2 ( )

Visualizations: ______________

Today's thought: ______________

______________

______________

Date: ______________ Completed 1 ( ) 2 ( )

Visualizations: ______________

Today's thought: ______________

______________

______________

Date: ______________ Completed 1 ( ) 2 ( )

Visualizations: ______________

Today's thought: ______________

______________

______________

Date: ______________ Completed 1 ( ) 2 ( )

Visualizations: ______________

Today's thought: ______________

______________

______________

Date: ________________ Completed 1 (  ) 2 (  )

Visualizations: ____________________________________

Today's thought: __________________________________

______________________________________________________

______________________________________________________

Date: ________________ Completed 1 (  ) 2 (  )

Visualizations: ____________________________________

Today's thought: __________________________________

______________________________________________________

______________________________________________________

Date: ________________ Completed 1 (  ) 2 (  )

Visualizations: ____________________________________

Today's thought: __________________________________

______________________________________________________

______________________________________________________

Date: ________________ Completed 1 (  ) 2 (  )

Visualizations: ____________________________________

Today's thought: __________________________________

______________________________________________________

______________________________________________________

Date: ____________ Completed 1 ( ) 2 ( )

Visualizations: ____________

Today's thought: ____________

Date: ____________ Completed 1 ( ) 2 ( )

Visualizations: ____________

Today's thought: ____________

Date: ____________ Completed 1 ( ) 2 ( )

Visualizations: ____________

Today's thought: ____________

Date: ____________ Completed 1 ( ) 2 ( )

Visualizations: ____________

Today's thought: ____________

Date: ______________ Completed 1 ( ) 2 ( )

Visualizations: ______________

Today's thought: ______________

______________

______________

Date: ______________ Completed 1 ( ) 2 ( )

Visualizations: ______________

Today's thought: ______________

______________

______________

Date: ______________ Completed 1 ( ) 2 ( )

Visualizations: ______________

Today's thought: ______________

______________

______________

Date: ______________ Completed 1 ( ) 2 ( )

Visualizations: ______________

Today's thought: ______________

______________

______________

Date: ____________ Completed 1 ( ) 2 ( )

Visualizations: ____________

Today's thought: ____________

Date: ____________ Completed 1 ( ) 2 ( )

Visualizations: ____________

Today's thought: ____________

Date: ____________ Completed 1 ( ) 2 ( )

Visualizations: ____________

Today's thought: ____________

Date: ____________ Completed 1 ( ) 2 ( )

Visualizations: ____________

Today's thought: ____________

Date: ____________ Completed 1 ( ) 2 ( )

Visualizations: ____________

Today's thought: ____________

____________

____________

Date: ____________ Completed 1 ( ) 2 ( )

Visualizations: ____________

Today's thought: ____________

____________

____________

Date: ____________ Completed 1 ( ) 2 ( )

Visualizations: ____________

Today's thought: ____________

____________

____________

Date: ____________ Completed 1 ( ) 2 ( )

Visualizations: ____________

Today's thought: ____________

____________

____________

Date: ______________ Completed 1 ( ) 2 ( )

Visualizations: ______________

Today's thought: ______________

______________

______________

Date: ______________ Completed 1 ( ) 2 ( )

Visualizations: ______________

Today's thought: ______________

______________

______________

Date: ______________ Completed 1 ( ) 2 ( )

Visualizations: ______________

Today's thought: ______________

______________

______________

Date: ______________ Completed 1 ( ) 2 ( )

Visualizations: ______________

Today's thought: ______________

______________

______________

Date: ________________ Completed 1 ( ) 2 ( )

Visualizations: ________________________________

Today's thought: ________________________________

________________________________________________

________________________________________________

Date: ________________ Completed 1 ( ) 2 ( )

Visualizations: ________________________________

Today's thought: ________________________________

________________________________________________

________________________________________________

Date: ________________ Completed 1 ( ) 2 ( )

Visualizations: ________________________________

Today's thought: ________________________________

________________________________________________

________________________________________________

Date: ________________ Completed 1 ( ) 2 ( )

Visualizations: ________________________________

Today's thought: ________________________________

________________________________________________

________________________________________________

Date: ______________ Completed 1 (  ) 2 (  )

Visualizations: ______________________

Today's thought: ______________________

______________________________________

______________________________________

Date: ______________ Completed 1 (  ) 2 (  )

Visualizations: ______________________

Today's thought: ______________________

______________________________________

______________________________________

Date: ______________ Completed 1 (  ) 2 (  )

Visualizations: ______________________

Today's thought: ______________________

______________________________________

______________________________________

Date: ______________ Completed 1 (  ) 2 (  )

Visualizations: ______________________

Today's thought: ______________________

______________________________________

______________________________________

Date: ______________ Completed 1 ( ) 2 ( )

Visualizations: ______________

Today's thought: ______________

______________

______________

Date: ______________ Completed 1 ( ) 2 ( )

Visualizations: ______________

Today's thought: ______________

______________

______________

Date: ______________ Completed 1 ( ) 2 ( )

Visualizations: ______________

Today's thought: ______________

______________

______________

Date: ______________ Completed 1 ( ) 2 ( )

Visualizations: ______________

Today's thought: ______________

______________

______________

Date: __________ Completed 1 ( ) 2 ( )

Visualizations: __________

Today's thought: __________

Date: __________ Completed 1 ( ) 2 ( )

Visualizations: __________

Today's thought: __________

Date: __________ Completed 1 ( ) 2 ( )

Visualizations: __________

Today's thought: __________

Date: __________ Completed 1 ( ) 2 ( )

Visualizations: __________

Today's thought: __________

Date: ____________________ Completed 1 (  ) 2 (  )

Visualizations: ________________________________

Today's thought: ______________________________

______________________________________________

______________________________________________

Date: ____________________ Completed 1 (  ) 2 (  )

Visualizations: ________________________________

Today's thought: ______________________________

______________________________________________

______________________________________________

Date: ____________________ Completed 1 (  ) 2 (  )

Visualizations: ________________________________

Today's thought: ______________________________

______________________________________________

______________________________________________

Date: ____________________ Completed 1 (  ) 2 (  )

Visualizations: ________________________________

Today's thought: ______________________________

______________________________________________

______________________________________________

Date: ______________ Completed 1 ( ) 2 ( )

Visualizations: ______________________________

Today's thought: ______________________________

______________________________

______________________________

Date: ______________ Completed 1 ( ) 2 ( )

Visualizations: ______________________________

Today's thought: ______________________________

______________________________

______________________________

Date: ______________ Completed 1 ( ) 2 ( )

Visualizations: ______________________________

Today's thought: ______________________________

______________________________

______________________________

Date: ______________ Completed 1 ( ) 2 ( )

Visualizations: ______________________________

Today's thought: ______________________________

______________________________

______________________________

Date: ________________ Completed 1 ( ) 2 ( )

Visualizations: ________________________

Today's thought: ________________________

________________________________________

________________________________________

Date: ________________ Completed 1 ( ) 2 ( )

Visualizations: ________________________

Today's thought: ________________________

________________________________________

________________________________________

Date: ________________ Completed 1 ( ) 2 ( )

Visualizations: ________________________

Today's thought: ________________________

________________________________________

________________________________________

Date: ________________ Completed 1 ( ) 2 ( )

Visualizations: ________________________

Today's thought: ________________________

________________________________________

________________________________________

Date: __________ Completed 1 (  ) 2 (  )

Visualizations: __________

Today's thought: __________

Date: __________ Completed 1 (  ) 2 (  )

Visualizations: __________

Today's thought: __________

Date: __________ Completed 1 (  ) 2 (  )

Visualizations: __________

Today's thought: __________

Date: __________ Completed 1 (  ) 2 (  )

Visualizations: __________

Today's thought: __________

Date: ____________ Completed 1 ( ) 2 ( )

Visualizations: ____________

Today's thought: ____________

____________

____________

Date: ____________ Completed 1 ( ) 2 ( )

Visualizations: ____________

Today's thought: ____________

____________

____________

Date: ____________ Completed 1 ( ) 2 ( )

Visualizations: ____________

Today's thought: ____________

____________

____________

Date: ____________ Completed 1 ( ) 2 ( )

Visualizations: ____________

Today's thought: ____________

____________

____________

Date: ______________ Completed 1 ( ) 2 ( )

Visualizations: ______________

Today's thought: ______________

______________

______________

Date: ______________ Completed 1 ( ) 2 ( )

Visualizations: ______________

Today's thought: ______________

______________

______________

Date: ______________ Completed 1 ( ) 2 ( )

Visualizations: ______________

Today's thought: ______________

______________

______________

Date: ______________ Completed 1 ( ) 2 ( )

Visualizations: ______________

Today's thought: ______________

______________

______________

Date: ________________ Completed 1 ( ) 2 ( )

Visualizations: ____________________________

Today's thought: ____________________________

____________________________________________

____________________________________________

Date: ________________ Completed 1 ( ) 2 ( )

Visualizations: ____________________________

Today's thought: ____________________________

____________________________________________

____________________________________________

Date: ________________ Completed 1 ( ) 2 ( )

Visualizations: ____________________________

Today's thought: ____________________________

____________________________________________

____________________________________________

Date: ________________ Completed 1 ( ) 2 ( )

Visualizations: ____________________________

Today's thought: ____________________________

____________________________________________

____________________________________________

Date: ______________ Completed 1 ( ) 2 ( )

Visualizations: ______________

Today's thought: ______________

______________

______________

Date: ______________ Completed 1 ( ) 2 ( )

Visualizations: ______________

Today's thought: ______________

______________

______________

Date: ______________ Completed 1 ( ) 2 ( )

Visualizations: ______________

Today's thought: ______________

______________

______________

Date: ______________ Completed 1 ( ) 2 ( )

Visualizations: ______________

Today's thought: ______________

______________

______________

Date: ________________ Completed 1 ( ) 2 ( )

Visualizations: ______________________________

Today's thought: ______________________________

______________________________________________

______________________________________________

Date: ________________ Completed 1 ( ) 2 ( )

Visualizations: ______________________________

Today's thought: ______________________________

______________________________________________

______________________________________________

Date: ________________ Completed 1 ( ) 2 ( )

Visualizations: ______________________________

Today's thought: ______________________________

______________________________________________

______________________________________________

Date: ________________ Completed 1 ( ) 2 ( )

Visualizations: ______________________________

Today's thought: ______________________________

______________________________________________

______________________________________________

Date: ______________ Completed 1 ( ) 2 ( )

Visualizations: ______________________________

Today's thought: ______________________________

______________________________

______________________________

Date: ______________ Completed 1 ( ) 2 ( )

Visualizations: ______________________________

Today's thought: ______________________________

______________________________

______________________________

Date: ______________ Completed 1 ( ) 2 ( )

Visualizations: ______________________________

Today's thought: ______________________________

______________________________

______________________________

Date: ______________ Completed 1 ( ) 2 ( )

Visualizations: ______________________________

Today's thought: ______________________________

______________________________

______________________________

Date: ______________ Completed 1 (  ) 2 (  )

Visualizations: ______________________________

Today's thought: ______________________________

______________________________________________

______________________________________________

Date: ______________ Completed 1 (  ) 2 (  )

Visualizations: ______________________________

Today's thought: ______________________________

______________________________________________

______________________________________________

Date: ______________ Completed 1 (  ) 2 (  )

Visualizations: ______________________________

Today's thought: ______________________________

______________________________________________

______________________________________________

Date: ______________ Completed 1 (  ) 2 (  )

Visualizations: ______________________________

Today's thought: ______________________________

______________________________________________

______________________________________________

Date: ________________ Completed 1 ( ) 2 ( )

Visualizations: ________________

Today's thought: ________________

________________

________________

Date: ________________ Completed 1 ( ) 2 ( )

Visualizations: ________________

Today's thought: ________________

________________

________________

Date: ________________ Completed 1 ( ) 2 ( )

Visualizations: ________________

Today's thought: ________________

________________

________________

Date: ________________ Completed 1 ( ) 2 ( )

Visualizations: ________________

Today's thought: ________________

________________

________________

Date: __________ Completed 1 ( ) 2 ( )

Visualizations: __________

Today's thought: __________

Date: __________ Completed 1 ( ) 2 ( )

Visualizations: __________

Today's thought: __________

Date: __________ Completed 1 ( ) 2 ( )

Visualizations: __________

Today's thought: __________

Date: __________ Completed 1 ( ) 2 ( )

Visualizations: __________

Today's thought: __________

Date: __________ Completed 1 ( ) 2 ( )

Visualizations: __________

Today's thought: __________

Date: __________ Completed 1 ( ) 2 ( )

Visualizations: __________

Today's thought: __________

Date: __________ Completed 1 ( ) 2 ( )

Visualizations: __________

Today's thought: __________

Date: __________ Completed 1 ( ) 2 ( )

Visualizations: __________

Today's thought: __________

Date: ______________ Completed 1 ( ) 2 ( )

Visualizations: ______________________

Today's thought: ______________________

______________________________________

______________________________________

Date: ______________ Completed 1 ( ) 2 ( )

Visualizations: ______________________

Today's thought: ______________________

______________________________________

______________________________________

Date: ______________ Completed 1 ( ) 2 ( )

Visualizations: ______________________

Today's thought: ______________________

______________________________________

______________________________________

Date: ______________ Completed 1 ( ) 2 ( )

Visualizations: ______________________

Today's thought: ______________________

______________________________________

______________________________________

Date: ______________ Completed 1 ( ) 2 ( )

Visualizations: ______________

Today's thought: ______________

______________

______________

Date: ______________ Completed 1 ( ) 2 ( )

Visualizations: ______________

Today's thought: ______________

______________

______________

Date: ______________ Completed 1 ( ) 2 ( )

Visualizations: ______________

Today's thought: ______________

______________

______________

Date: ______________ Completed 1 ( ) 2 ( )

Visualizations: ______________

Today's thought: ______________

______________

______________

Date: ______________ Completed 1 ( ) 2 ( )

Visualizations: ______________________________

Today's thought: ______________________________

______________________________________________

______________________________________________

Date: ______________ Completed 1 ( ) 2 ( )

Visualizations: ______________________________

Today's thought: ______________________________

______________________________________________

______________________________________________

Date: ______________ Completed 1 ( ) 2 ( )

Visualizations: ______________________________

Today's thought: ______________________________

______________________________________________

______________________________________________

Date: ______________ Completed 1 ( ) 2 ( )

Visualizations: ______________________________

Today's thought: ______________________________

______________________________________________

______________________________________________

Date: __________ Completed 1 (  ) 2 (  )

Visualizations: __________

Today's thought: __________

Date: __________ Completed 1 (  ) 2 (  )

Visualizations: __________

Today's thought: __________

Date: __________ Completed 1 (  ) 2 (  )

Visualizations: __________

Today's thought: __________

Date: __________ Completed 1 (  ) 2 (  )

Visualizations: __________

Today's thought: __________

Date: ________________ Completed 1 (  ) 2 (  )

Visualizations: ________________

Today's thought: ________________

________________

________________

Date: ________________ Completed 1 (  ) 2 (  )

Visualizations: ________________

Today's thought: ________________

________________

________________

Date: ________________ Completed 1 (  ) 2 (  )

Visualizations: ________________

Today's thought: ________________

________________

________________

Date: ________________ Completed 1 (  ) 2 (  )

Visualizations: ________________

Today's thought: ________________

________________

________________

Date: ______________ Completed 1 (  ) 2 (  )

Visualizations: ______________

Today's thought: ______________

Date: ______________ Completed 1 (  ) 2 (  )

Visualizations: ______________

Today's thought: ______________

Date: ______________ Completed 1 (  ) 2 (  )

Visualizations: ______________

Today's thought: ______________

Date: ______________ Completed 1 (  ) 2 (  )

Visualizations: ______________

Today's thought: ______________

Date: ______________ Completed 1 (  ) 2 (  )

Visualizations: ______________________________

Today's thought: ______________________________

______________________________________________

______________________________________________

Date: ______________ Completed 1 (  ) 2 (  )

Visualizations: ______________________________

Today's thought: ______________________________

______________________________________________

______________________________________________

Date: ______________ Completed 1 (  ) 2 (  )

Visualizations: ______________________________

Today's thought: ______________________________

______________________________________________

______________________________________________

Date: ______________ Completed 1 (  ) 2 (  )

Visualizations: ______________________________

Today's thought: ______________________________

______________________________________________

______________________________________________

Date: ____________ Completed 1 (  ) 2 (  )

Visualizations: ____________

Today's thought: ____________

Date: ____________ Completed 1 (  ) 2 (  )

Visualizations: ____________

Today's thought: ____________

Date: ____________ Completed 1 (  ) 2 (  )

Visualizations: ____________

Today's thought: ____________

Date: ____________ Completed 1 (  ) 2 (  )

Visualizations: ____________

Today's thought: ____________

Date: ____________ Completed 1 ( ) 2 ( )

Visualizations: ____________

Today's thought: ____________

____________

____________

Date: ____________ Completed 1 ( ) 2 ( )

Visualizations: ____________

Today's thought: ____________

____________

____________

Date: ____________ Completed 1 ( ) 2 ( )

Visualizations: ____________

Today's thought: ____________

____________

____________

Date: ____________ Completed 1 ( ) 2 ( )

Visualizations: ____________

Today's thought: ____________

____________

____________

Date: ____________ Completed 1 ( ) 2 ( )

Visualizations: ____________

Today's thought: ____________

____________

____________

Date: ____________ Completed 1 ( ) 2 ( )

Visualizations: ____________

Today's thought: ____________

____________

____________

Date: ____________ Completed 1 ( ) 2 ( )

Visualizations: ____________

Today's thought: ____________

____________

____________

Date: ____________ Completed 1 ( ) 2 ( )

Visualizations: ____________

Today's thought: ____________

____________

____________

Date: ________________ Completed 1 (  ) 2 (  )

Visualizations: ________________________________

Today's thought: ________________________________

________________________________________________

________________________________________________

Date: ________________ Completed 1 (  ) 2 (  )

Visualizations: ________________________________

Today's thought: ________________________________

________________________________________________

________________________________________________

Date: ________________ Completed 1 (  ) 2 (  )

Visualizations: ________________________________

Today's thought: ________________________________

________________________________________________

________________________________________________

Date: ________________ Completed 1 (  ) 2 (  )

Visualizations: ________________________________

Today's thought: ________________________________

________________________________________________

________________________________________________

Date: ______________ Completed 1 ( ) 2 ( )

Visualizations: ______________________

Today's thought: ______________________

______________________________________

______________________________________

Date: ______________ Completed 1 ( ) 2 ( )

Visualizations: ______________________

Today's thought: ______________________

______________________________________

______________________________________

Date: ______________ Completed 1 ( ) 2 ( )

Visualizations: ______________________

Today's thought: ______________________

______________________________________

______________________________________

Date: ______________ Completed 1 ( ) 2 ( )

Visualizations: ______________________

Today's thought: ______________________

______________________________________

______________________________________

Date: ____________ Completed 1 (  ) 2 (  )

Visualizations: ____________

Today's thought: ____________

____________

____________

Date: ____________ Completed 1 (  ) 2 (  )

Visualizations: ____________

Today's thought: ____________

____________

____________

Date: ____________ Completed 1 (  ) 2 (  )

Visualizations: ____________

Today's thought: ____________

____________

____________

Date: ____________ Completed 1 (  ) 2 (  )

Visualizations: ____________

Today's thought: ____________

____________

____________

Date: ______________ Completed 1 ( ) 2 ( )

Visualizations: ______________

Today's thought: ______________

Date: ______________ Completed 1 ( ) 2 ( )

Visualizations: ______________

Today's thought: ______________

Date: ______________ Completed 1 ( ) 2 ( )

Visualizations: ______________

Today's thought: ______________

Date: ______________ Completed 1 ( ) 2 ( )

Visualizations: ______________

Today's thought: ______________

Date: ____________ Completed 1 ( ) 2 ( )

Visualizations: ____________

Today's thought: ____________

____________

____________

Date: ____________ Completed 1 ( ) 2 ( )

Visualizations: ____________

Today's thought: ____________

____________

____________

Date: ____________ Completed 1 ( ) 2 ( )

Visualizations: ____________

Today's thought: ____________

____________

____________

Date: ____________ Completed 1 ( ) 2 ( )

Visualizations: ____________

Today's thought: ____________

____________

____________

Date: ______________ Completed 1 ( ) 2 ( )

Visualizations: ______________

Today's thought: ______________

______________

______________

Date: ______________ Completed 1 ( ) 2 ( )

Visualizations: ______________

Today's thought: ______________

______________

______________

Date: ______________ Completed 1 ( ) 2 ( )

Visualizations: ______________

Today's thought: ______________

______________

______________

Date: ______________ Completed 1 ( ) 2 ( )

Visualizations: ______________

Today's thought: ______________

______________

______________

Date: ______________ Completed 1 ( ) 2 ( )

Visualizations: ______________

Today's thought: ______________

______________

______________

Date: ______________ Completed 1 ( ) 2 ( )

Visualizations: ______________

Today's thought: ______________

______________

______________

Date: ______________ Completed 1 ( ) 2 ( )

Visualizations: ______________

Today's thought: ______________

______________

______________

Date: ______________ Completed 1 ( ) 2 ( )

Visualizations: ______________

Today's thought: ______________

______________

______________

*Order Your Next*

# *My Book of Life*

## TODAY!

Those of you who've picked up on **The Guardian Code** already understand. This isn't just a book; it's a way of life. And once you know the secrets of **The Guardian Code**, it will be impossible for you not to live by them.

What *My Book of Life* does, is make it easier for you to put them into practice every single day. And they're set up as small, easy-reference books that you can carry with you in your pocket, purse, attaché or backpack.

You get two a year when you order here. And once you do, you'll find out that they become so much a part of your life, you'll never want to be without them. Consider them "Your Guardian Reference" to instant awareness…and it's something you've always had. (And of course, if you're one of those eBook mavens who likes to download everything, it's also available on Amazon [Kindle] and Barnes& Noble [Nook] as well.)

Order hardcover copies of *My Book of Life* from:

**www.SteveShenk.com**

Soft cover copies, ISBN: 978-1-60414-729-6, are available from:

**www.SteveShenk.com**
**www.Amazon.com**
**www.BarnesAndNoble.com**
**& other online retailers**

# ABOUT THE AUTHOR

Steve Shenk is a philosopher, educator, noted food expert, and 30-year entrepreneur. As a voice of reason on matters of relationships, happiness and prosperity, Steve's book, THE GUARDIAN CODE: It's Not Your Fault [And I Can Prove It!], delves into his philosophies of life and relationships. THE GUARDIAN CODE was written to share the secrets to finding the magnificence within each of us. The book is discussed on his weekly radio/Internet T V talk show of the same name. He is also a frequent guest of some of America's favorite talk show programs.

Steve feels that every individual desperately needs to know how to take control of their lives, not only to survive, but to prosper and enjoy fulfilling relationships. In a time when it seems all life is crashing down around each of us, Steve shares his insights with the goal of helping each and every one of us to realize the magnificence and grandeur of who we are.

Raised by a father who was virtually an "animal whisperer," horses have been a part of his life since he started riding at age three. Steve has a sense and a love for animals that verges on extraordinary. In fact, his dog, Lexi, joins him at the office every day.

**www.SteveShenk.com**

www.ingramcontent.com/pod-product-compliance
Lightning Source LLC
Chambersburg PA
CBHW071012120726
47910CB00004B/1485

* 9 7 8 1 6 0 4 1 4 7 2 9 2 *